SHOCK

Shelly in Shock

ISBN 978-0-9954804-0-7
First published 2016 by Emotional Logic Publishing
Emotional Logic Centre, South Highlands,
Blachford Road, Ivybridge,
Devon PL21 0AD

Text © 2016 Sarah Lakey
Illustrations © 2016 Bradley Goodwin

Printed in the United Kingdom

All rights reserved. No part of this book shall be reproduced or transmitted in any form or by any means, electronic or mechanical, including photocopying, recording or by any information retrieval system, without written permission from the publisher.

www.elpublishing.org.uk

The sun shimmered over the Savannah as Shelly the tortoise sat under the cooling shade of her favourite tree, right next to her favourite yellow flowers.

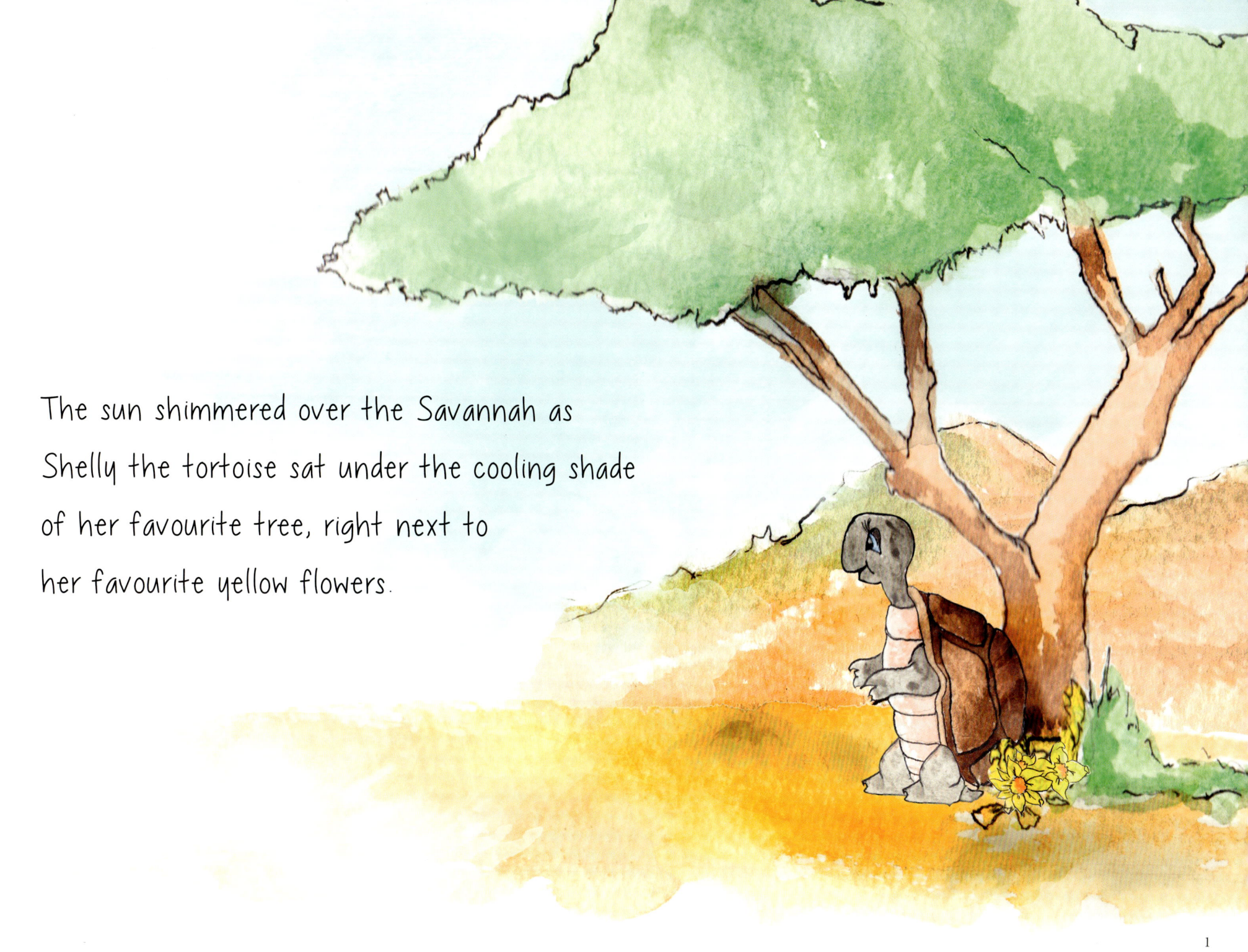

She watched her friends play with a huge, happy SMILE spreading across her face.

Monte the monkey ZOOMed around all of the other animals playing chase, while Shelly was in her happy place by the tree. She was happy not joining in because she preferred to be at tortoise speed... slow or completely stopped!

Shelly rested. Shelly watched.
　　Shelly dozed. Shelly smiled.

Shelly breathed in the delicious sweet scent of the beautiful, bright flowers when...

Bzzzzzzzzzzzz

"Ouch!"

Bzzzzzzzzzzzz

"Oh no! What happened? Oh no!"
A large buzzing bee had landed on Shelly's nose.
With a zing and a ding, she felt the sting!

Shelly immediately hid in her shell.
She couldn't think what to do.

Her nose turned from pink to red to swollen.

Her friends didn't see –
they were too busy playing!

Shelly began to tremble and shake. She could hear her friends laughing and playing. They were so near but they felt so far away. Shelly felt so alone, so small…

PLOP!

Huge tears rolled down from her eyes to her sore red nose.

When anything surprised Shelly, she would always take fright and hide in her shell. But then she missed out on all of the fun.

The warm sunlit sky began to change and deepen to rich reds and pinks.

Soon her friends left for home.

"Bye, Shelly!"

"Night, night!" they all called.

The animals thought she must be fast asleep because they didn't hear her little voice stutter out. . . .

"P-p-p-p-please... help me?"

Shelly wasn't sleeping at all. In fact, she was lonely and worried. She wanted to be with her friends. Shelly thought back to earlier that day...

The next day, the sun rose high in the sky, and all the animals came out to play but...

Shelly was still inside her shell!
Still worrying! Still filled with fear!

But then she had an amazing idea...

I'll live in my shell FOREVER! Then I'll be safe. The outside world is too dangerous for me!

But then she realised what that would mean.

"Oh no," she thought.

"That won't do at all because I'll never get to see my friends again, or play with them, or sit by my favourite flowers, or…"

NO FUN

NO FRIENDS

It seemed hopeless.

She didn't know what to do!

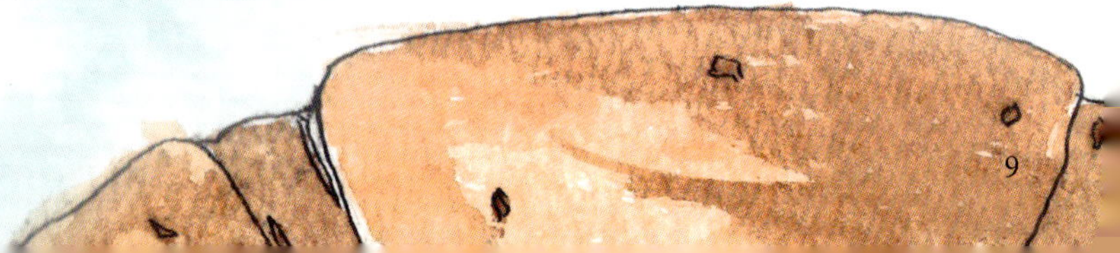

Zora the zebra, Monte the monkey and Ollie the ostrich all tried to encourage Shelly out to play. They became worried too. They tried to persuade her out with juicy leaves, yellow flowers and even Monte's bananas! But nothing helped her to stop being frightened.

Shelly remained in her shell.

Zora hated seeing her friend so sad. She thought for a while and then suggested, "Let's get Lisimba. He'll know exactly what to do."

"Great idea," agreed Ollie, who hurried off into the bush on his long legs in search of Lisimba the friendly lion.

As soon as he heard the news, Lisimba came. He was brave, strong and wise. He was the king of the Savannah after all!

Monte leaped up and down in the air as he exclaimed to Lisimba,

"Oh my gosh!"

"Can you believe it, Lisimba! She's been in her shell since yesterday afternoon!

YESTERDAY AFTERNOON!"

"She won't come out to play," said Ollie ostrich.

"She won't even sit by her favourite flowers," said Zora.

"Mmmmmmmmmmmm," murmured Lisimba.

"Sounds like shock to me."

"Oh no. Oh no – this isn't good!" cried Ollie.

"I wonder if she is hiding from something?" continued Lisimba. "She probably feels safer in her shell, but now she doesn't know what to do next!"

"That sounds bad," said Zora, "Oh... really bad!"

Lisimba looked at Shelly's safe shell and slowly gathered everyone close around. "Well, friends, I know it sounds bad, and it definitely feels bad, but shock can be really useful too."

Lisimba looked at the puzzled faces around Shelly. He knew he needed to explain...

"You see, when you have a feeling deep inside that makes you think, 'What should I do? Help! I can't do this!' it means you should

STOP!

Shock feelings mean something really

IMPORTANT

is happening.

Right at that moment, you **MUST** find a safe place to have a really good think — a place where you can work it all out."

"Shelly has found a safe place, but she hasn't really started to think yet. Perhaps she could find a kind friend or a safe grown-up to tell them what happened."

Then, perhaps they could plan together what to do to **move on from the safe place.**"

During all of this, Shelly quietly listened from deep within her shell. Hearing Lisimba's voice, she started to think.

> Maybe I could do something just a little bit risky.

She carefully peeped her nose out of her shell.

Feeling braver now, Shelly peeped out a little further, until she could look straight at Lisimba.

"It's OK Shelly," encouraged Lisimba. "Whatever shocked you must be far away by now."

"Oh no! Oh my!" exclaimed Ollie. "What's that on the end of your nose?"

"I was stung by a bee!"

wailed Shelly.

"I didn't know what to do. I didn't feel safe, so I hid in my shell. That helped for a little while, but hiding didn't solve the problem at all."

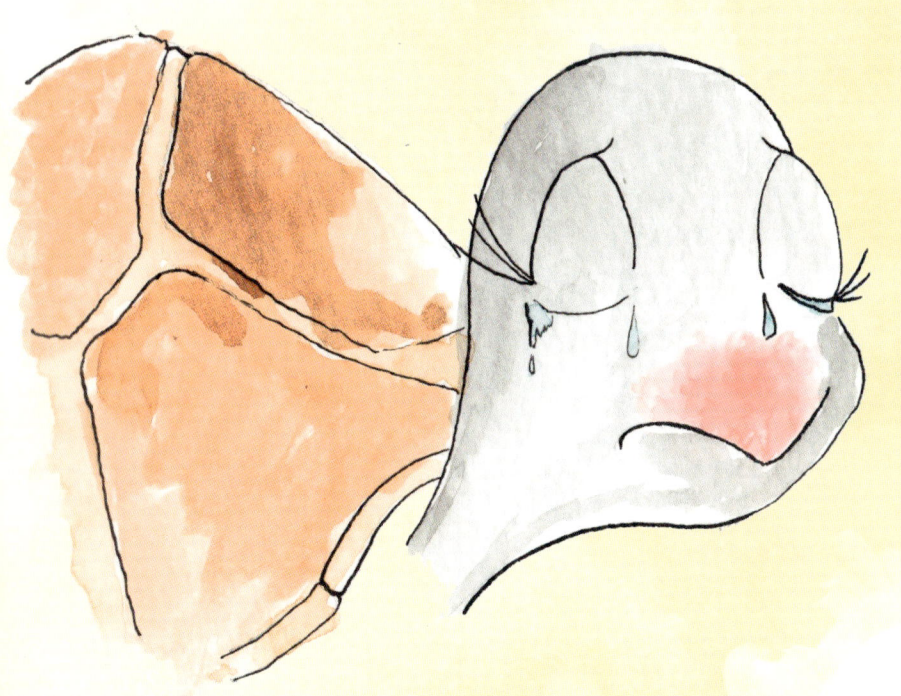

Lisimba tapped Shelly's shell.

"That is a great place to think more clearly, Shelly. In there you could ask yourself a very important question... 'When I felt shocked what was I upset that i'd lost?'

"When you can answer that question," explained Lisimba, "you can plan what you could DO next to move on. If you don't ask that question, you will end up feeling stuck!"

Shelly gazed from one friend to another, and feeling safe with them, it all came tumbling out... "I lost..."

My happy day.

My favourite tree.

Feeling safe.

My friends to play with.

My healthy nose.

"Oh! That's so many things to lose!" Shelly cried, as she flopped down and immediately disappeared into her shell again.

All the animals looked worried as they turned away from Lisimba to look at the silent shell.

"It's all right, Shelly," soothed Lisimba. "It's fine to feel upset, but now you have named what you've lost, you can make a plan to get one thing back!"

"Make a plan? Make a plan?" asked Monte, bobbing from side to side.

Lisimba bent down to where Shelly's head had been. His deep voice echoed inside her shell.

"Come on, Shelly, choose just one thing that you've lost that you CAN get back."

Shelly peeped out once more, "Just one?"

All the animals, even Monte, sat still with puzzled faces and looked back at Lisimba.

"Just one?" their faces seemed to say.

Lisimba nodded.

Shelly popped her head out of her shell in surprise.

"Yes," said Lisimba, very wisely.

"Just one first, and then some of the others next…"

"I… my, my… sunny… day," stuttered Shelly.
"I want to get back my sunny day. I could go and sit by the trees next to the cool river. There are not so many bees there."

All the friends suddenly cheered!

"What a fantastic idea!" said Zora.

"We could come and play there too."

Shelly beamed, and began to walk slowly towards the river. "Thank you for talking to me, Lisimba," she said, as she passed by his great paws.

"Wonderful, wonderful!" roared Lisimba. "When you choose to get things back, you'll start to feel better again."

Shelly stretched her legs out even further, as she walked more and more confidently towards the river bank.

"Oh wow!"

"I chose to get back my sunny day, and now I've got my friends back too, and a place to play, and a chance to doze, and somewhere cool for my nose."

As Shelly approached, Terry the tortoise was sitting by the river bank.

"Hi Shelly!" Terry called.

"What a lovely surprise to see you today."

Shelly played "bump the shells" with Terry.

She had an AMAZING time by the river bank.

As the sun set, Shelly settled down to sleep in her shell.
She remembered all that she had learned.

Her shock had been useful to
   get her to her safe place,
      but now she knew how to plan
         there too, and how to move on again.

Lisimba had made even taking little risks feel safer.

Shelly's special friends had
   encouraged her too. She drifted
      off to sleep, looking forward to
         more fun the next day . . .